Devotions

with selections from

A Painter's Bestiary
and 14 drawings from Intentions

text and art

by

BASIL KING

Stop Press • London • 1997

Some of the selections from *The Painter's Bestiary* first appeared in the following poetry magazines: *The St. Mark's Poetry Project Newsletter*, *Lift*, *Texture*, *lyric &*, *C.A.T.H.A.Y.*, and *Giants Play Well in the Drizzle...* 5/8/98

"The Yellow Christ" was anthologized in *In the West of Ireland*, Enright House, 1992.

The fourteen pencil drawings, "*Intentions*," reproduced in this book, were created in 1990.

Also published in a limited signed edition of 50 copies (ISBN 0 9529961 5 4)

ISBN 0 9529961 4 6

Published by
Stop Press
London

Printed in the U.K.
by CPI

"The man who has not realized the difficulty of art," said Chardin in 1765, "never does anything worthwhile; the man who realizes it too soon, does nothing at all."

Devotions

By way of introduction. . .

These are the devotions of painters: Pollock, Vermeer, Seurat, Gorky, Holbein...Morandi, Degas, Lautrec, and Franz Kline. Manet and Poussin, Cezanne, Monet, Van Gogh. They are considered as a devotion by another painter, Basil King, who has been called by the poet Theodore Enslin, "our Vasari". . .

If you know the works of these artists you can float their images as you read; if you do not, you nevertheless know something of devotion from somewhere else. . .

The second half of this book is a related effort: the painting and its painter as a wonder to be celebrated just as creatures were by the creators of medieval bestiaries. Then, the intention was exemplary. Here, an intention becomes intentions: there is no catalog; instead, a veil between viewer and viewed is deliberately dissolved. . .

DEVOTIONS

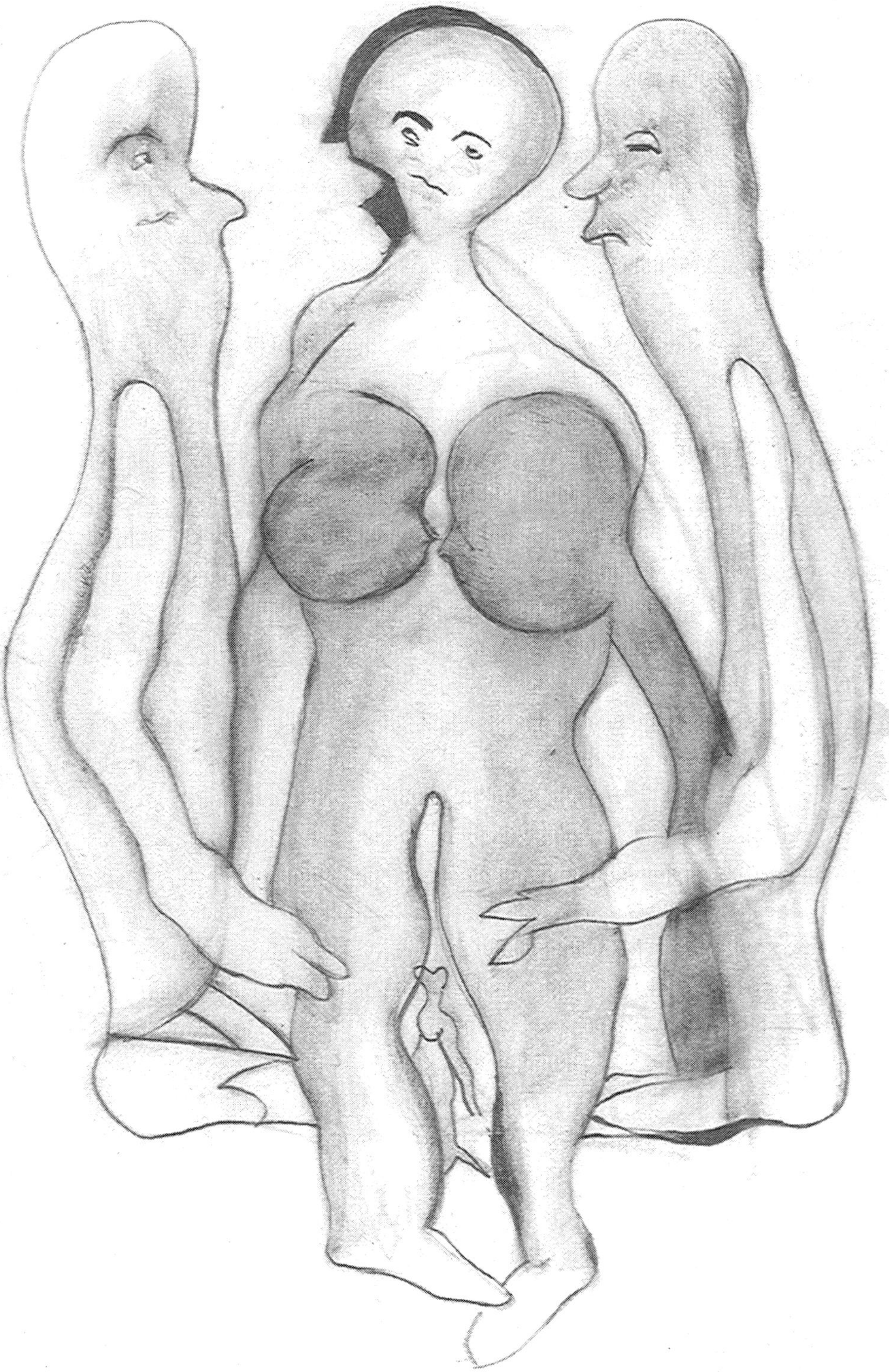

Jackson Pollock (1912-1956)

Deep and scented and lavender-misted. Male and female. Like rain falling from the sky to the ground. Falling from the sky to the ground. See how devotion repeats itself in forms that give new meaning to place. And in the harshness of Jackson Pollock's northern temperament, he scorns accident. So be it. If in the strength of his passion he made a tropic of cruelty, so be it. The weather instructs the rain and, like grass, it is beholden. And if, like rain, devotion repeats itself in forms that give new meaning to place, then stir those semi-precious things. They were fed into Mural and into Eyes in the Heat.

Monday begins another week. And the dream becomes The Deep and Scent and Lavender Mist. The wounded animal is gothic to The Blue Unconscious. Today I walk three thousand miles to eat at a table in London. Today, Pollock's 1946 Mural is as fresh as it was yesterday. Yesterday. Today, feed these semi-precious things into your palm. And repeat the weather's instructions to the rain and fall from the sky to the ground.

Echo. Totem I. Guardians of the Secret. Preamble. Like rain falling down from the sky to the ground. Four Opposites. Ritual. Ocean Greyness. Echo. Blue Poles. Black and White. Number 5. Convergence finds Search and Search finds its instructions. In Full Fathom Five, the key opens the door. And there is Monday. Monday begins another week.

Today looking at Pollock's work is like seeing something from very long ago that should have been instilled in us, that should complement us. Touch. The keys are still with us but our Blue Poles are harder and harder to trust. Powerful forces have deliberately worked overtime to make what can be spontaneous seem immature. Not even children are allowed innocence. Keats and Rimbaud are applauded but paid no attention to. The unknown is proven wanting and unneeded. Pollock's scent scent scent searches the interior and reminds us that there is bedrock.

Jan Vermeer (1632-1675)

And what of your house? Its walls and its doors. In your house, where is your bed? The table and chairs where you eat? Where do you read? Do you have enough wall space to hang paintings, drawings, maps, photographs? How many mirrors do you have? Do you look at yourself in the mirror? With or without your clothes on? Have you made love in front of a mirror? Is love something you associate with your home? with your paintings, drawings, and maps? Do you have more than one color on the walls of your house? Do you like to visit other people's houses and do you take note of what they have on their walls and where they sit and eat and read and sleep? Do you count how many mirrors they have? Do you look different when you see yourself in one of their mirrors?

A house is where we bring everything from the outside inside. And each morning or whenever we leave our houses, we take with us to the outside something that happened. Good or bad. Something happened even if we didn't move the furniture or look in the mirror or eat some food. Something happened and the narrative is our story. I saw her pour milk. I saw her put her necklace on. I saw her read a letter. The narrative has its song. Its little song.

Jan Vermeer sat when he painted. At eye level, he watched the women of his house read their letters, pour milk, rest.

Domesticity is the wildest. I insist. Light abstracts the simplest things. A pregnant woman stands by a table reading a letter. Behind her, on a wall of different whites there is a map. Another Dutch painter knew this painting when few knew Vermeer. Van Gogh was to say about Woman in Blue Reading a Letter:

"This strange painter's palette consists of blue, lemon-yellow, pearl-grey, black, and white." You can see the same colors in Girl in a Turban. The black background is vertical and frames the girl's face. She is about to say --. Vermeer's ladies keep to themselves and sometimes we are an intrusion. The girl is soft. A pearl. A hint of devotion. The woman is soft. Her blue jacket centers her between two dark blue chairs and separates her from the wall and the table. Is the letter from someone she loves?

These strange paintings. Cool. Mature. These self-contained moments refract and bring camera obscura to life. An open window. Music. You can hear it: music for contour. A high C for horn. A necklace. Vermeer color. The distance between things. An experiment so thoroughly simple that at first glance it's hard to see the differences. But this strange man painted what he saw and what he saw was different.

If the scholars are right and he was frugal, then his arrangements were brilliant. By moving the furniture into different rooms and positioning the ladies he created a world within his home. But unlike Vuillard he doesn't resort to closure. His intention is in front of him. A short story begins but never ends. Vermeer's punctuation, like his coloring, is impeccable. He tells us there is variety and the wonder of it is, it's transmittable.

Seurat / Vermeer

In Seurat (1859-1891), green curves. Shoulders slump. Trees stand.Vertical models pose. Outside it's summer, always summer. Red dots. Purple dots. The experiment. (Democracy?) Bathing at Asnieres, 1883-84. An Afternoon at La Grande Jatte, 1884-85. The work never stops. Seated Model, Back (study for The Model.) Seurat's Chromo-Luminarism: the back becomes a monument, every dot diffusing the contour.

There's a line that goes back to Vermeer. It's not a straight line. I'm not even sure about the curves. But Seurat and Vermeer walked into the same space at different times. They saw something different. For them light is not only at the edge of the object, it is inside and it is outside, and it's cool, mature. It's fuel.

Consider the alternative. If everything were sleight of hand, quicker than the eye, would we be able to feel our way around in the dark? Would we ever have a sense of where the edge is? Where would distance be? What would we do with color? Would we become malevolent?

I insist. Light abstracts the smallest things. It's easier to be alone when working. It's harder to eat alone. True -- False. With a large painting. With a small painting. With a surface that has much paint. With a surface that has a small quantity of paint.

True -- False. Eat with your fork. Some people won't pick up a piece of chicken and eat it off the bone. But Seurat and

Vermeer walked into the same space at different times. They saw something different. To them, light is not only at the edge of the object, it is inside and it is outside. And it's cool, mature. It's fuel. It's part of the natural world.

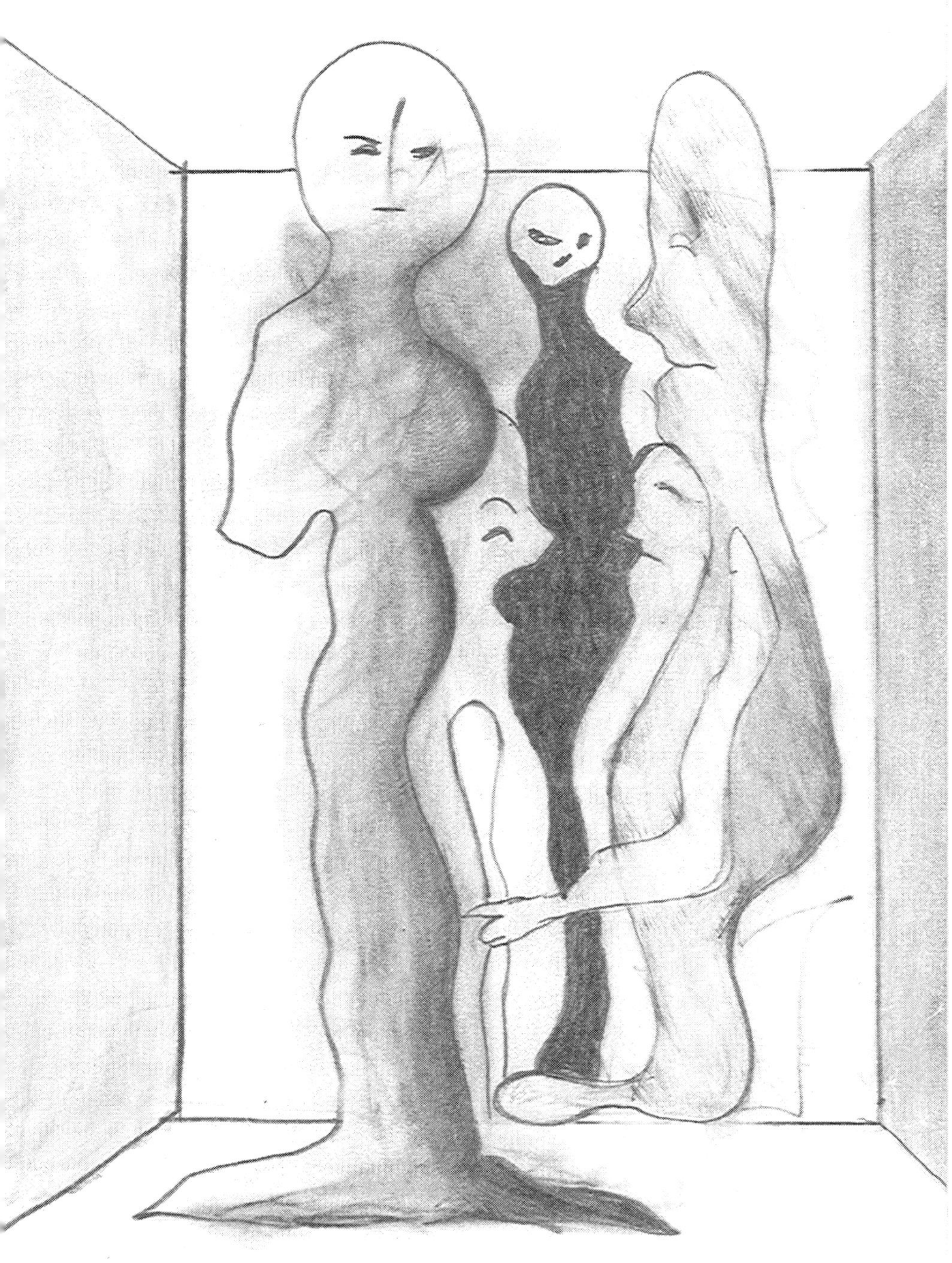

Gorky / Holbein

Black, white, with two different greens, some yellow, and a milky rosy red. These are the colors of Arshile Gorky's Last Painting (1948). Arshile Gorky, 1905-1948. Did anyone ever see Gorky draw? Agony. Waterfall. Drawing. Good Afternoon, Mrs. Lincoln. Drawing is an organ of contradiction. It is always new.

Holbein -- Hans Holbein the Younger, 1497-1543. The English saw what they paid for and they were lucky. He drew them as human beings. North and South melted into his crayons. Organic contradiction enabled him to achieve what Dürer had started.

Draw. The pencil slides. Draw. My automatic response is to keep going. Drawing. A still life on the table will not move. Europe is the museum. America, the attic. Picasso-- Miro-- Gorky slid them up and down the page until he found America. Draw. How My Mother's Embroidered Apron Unfolds in My Life. Draw. A Study of the Unattainable. Draw. Betrothal. Draw. Good Afternoon, Mrs. Lincoln.

Holbein left Switzerland in his early thirties for England with letters of recommendation from the scholar, Erasmus of Rotterdam. "The arts here are freezing," he was to write his friend, Sir Thomas More. Holbein, at the time, was becoming the "master of the German-speaking countries." The Reformation put a stop to that, almost put a stop to art. No more statues of saints in the churches. No more paintings as altar pieces. No luxury, no decoration in the home or church. All Popish idolatry. The Calvinists objected.

Vosdanig Manooy Adoian was born in 1905 in Turkish Armenia, and educated in the American mission school. His father deserted the family in 1908, fleeing from Turkish military service. In 1918, Adoian's mother died. And in 1920, he and his youngest sister made their way to America where they joined their father and two older sisters. When he was twenty-five, he adopted the name Arshille Gorky. He had a long and hard apprenticeship and, because of poverty, he was mostly self-taught.

To leave what is familiar--if it is as a fifteen-year-old boy as Gorky was when he left Turkish Armenia, or as a mature master, as Holbein was when he left Switzerland--takes courage, even if you are fleeing danger. The not-so-strong stay, as some did in Germany in the 1930's.

Migrate. To move from one country or place of abode to another with a view to residence. Birds and some other animals do it to breed. But these brave men had to migrate. Imagine a mirror and you are looking at yourself and you are upside down. Imagine Tintoretto is all space. Raphael looks like a Bauhaus lesson. And Ucello has become Mondrian's mentor. Look. You see something. There it is. It's upside down. It's inside out. And you've caught it. You know there's a contradiction. As the skin begins to cover the frame you see your face righting itself, and the eyes, ears, nose, and mouth are touched by a hand.

He called himself Arshille; and he remained Hans. The migration that took place when they crossed the waters has ended. After much discomfort, they begin to adopt and be adopted. They begin to accept and be accepted. To migrate is exciting. And to migrate can be frightening. It is not a vacation. You are not a tourist. You are The Liver is a Cock's Comb. Liver, a resident, a dweller, as a dweller, a liver in Brooklyn. The liver, regarded as the seat of passion or desire, discharges, and you are free to migrate.

Morandi

Oh, spirit dear! Warm my body so that I may have a good day. Oh, spirit, plant into my palm the shadows that have dried beneath the sand. Plant into my palms the still lifes and water colors that make me tremble. Spirit, you have engraved into me what I feel and now when I pass a house, a tree on this road that I am walking, it is not enough. I am beset by shadows. By flowers. By walls and tables. By faces I do not see. By fathers I do not know. Spirit, consider kindness. I need to rest. To drink and have something to eat. Consider. Consider my health. I need the sun. My palms want color. Summer's color melts the edges and the edges purr. Morandi's edges purr.

Giorgio Morandi (1890-1964) sleeps on a cot in the same room with his easel. His easel is caked with paint. He is a large man and most probably very strong. His work is not totally abstract, realistic, or surreal. His drawings are like notations for something that might be. And I am reminded that Chardin (1699-1779) touched upon this subject. A bottle, a table, and a wall. All objects are handled and organically become texture. I insist light abstracts the simplest things. Morandi takes advantage of it. There's the table and there's the wall, and there are the edges. I see no sacrifice. I see the artist doing what he wants. The accomplishment is enormous.

The bottle loses its symbol,
The dish remains empty,
The landscape has not one
single leaf. Water weathered
by color touches water.
Crayon touches paper and
the horizon line settles
between the table and the wall.
Nothing is negative. The
vases, dishes, and bottles have
become shadows that have
dried beneath the sand, are
planted into the palm,
and summer's color melts the edges.
The edges purr.
Morandi's edges purr.

Lautrec / Degas

It is common knowledge that Toulouse Lautrec (1864-1901) would live in a brothel for weeks and that he would draw and paint the women. It was the nineteenth century and he was a rich man. Thirty years older than Lautrec, Edgar Degas (1834-1917) drew, painted, and sculpted young women dancers. Both men drew and painted horses. Degas sculpted them. It was the nineteenth century, and neither man married. Did they want to? Was it that they were artists and women didn't want them? Lautrec was short and ugly but short and ugly men get married. And he was rich. The brothel was available to both men. Is that why they didn't marry? Or was it that they had particular ideas about women?

The Swan crosses the floor as if it were a merry-go-round. The Dance at the Moulin Rouge (1890). 1890--Van Gogh is dead. The lion never sleeps. The horse never eats. Solo and Duet. Toulouse and Lautrec. Henri Marie Raymond de Toulouse Lautrec traces his lineage back to Charlemagne. Traces. Traces. To the right of Utamaro stands Lautrec's white-bearded father. Hiroshige is busy. The printer's ink. The Dance at the Moulin Rouge.

This Swan wears a pink dress and a busy hat. Sometimes. Sometimes, a musician plays. Sometimes the dancers stand still and incubate. The Swan crosses the floor as if it were a merry-go-round. Grief wears a reddish hat and a green dress. And in the center rear, in a black cape, is Jane Avril. Everywhere there are men. Before. Before old age. Before pain. Before the Swan crosses the floor as if it were a merry-go-round, the dancers' frenzy attracts Lautrec. And before the crayon touches the table, he licks his lips. Wet. The shadow is wet. A bow crosses the cello. Time, she said, is lateral. The Swan crosses the floor as if it were on a merry-go-round. The shadow. Is wet. The dance. A bow crosses the cello. Time. She said. Is lateral. The dance is wet. The Swan crosses the floor as if she were on a merry-go-round.

I remember a painting by Degas I saw in his retrospective at the Metropolitan. It is called something like Peasant Girls Bathing in the Sea. There are three lovely naked young women bathing; in the background is a factory and smoke is bellowing from a chimney. It is sunset. It should have been romantic. But it isn't. It is the worst of the nineteenth century, the century when Japanese prints came to France, and of Marie Curie, of Pasteur, of Degas' painting. Three naked working girls washing after how many hours of work and still breathing fumes. They might give themselves to a man that night. Would he be as tired as they are? He'd remember her the next day and want her again. And maybe she'd want him. Or would she want the other young women and would they want to float together and have the sunset as the male?

Empathy. Degas was a working artist. Lautrec was a working artist. Folk art, primitive art, does something else. Folk art, primitive art, comes from somewhere else.

Ancient sculpted Venuses, for want of a better name, were sculpted by women for women. They could have worn them as amulets--some of the Venuses being one inch in height and having holes in them. Or they could have kept them where they slept or groomed themselves. I think older women gave them to younger women. Sometimes for protection, the older women having known what it was like to be swollen and to give birth. Or mothers gave them to their daughters. Empathy. Pride. Not all the Venuses are pregnant.

In Degas' and Lautrec's work, the art never dissolves. The younger and older women do not dissolve. The prostitutes and young dancers these men so harshly scrutinized with pen-- pencil-- oil-- and clay-- remain and some women sculpt and some wear amulets.

Franz Kline

Calligraphy is for lovers. Black. White. Like Dürer's prints. A practical message from home. To those who do not have a home. BLACK - WHITE. Together. Separated. Together they are a structure. Franz Kline (1910-1962) seems to have been able to follow Rembrandt and the Japanese calligraphers. He seems to have been able to stop at a moment's notice and then begin again. It is as Charles Olson said, "He who controls rhythm, controls" and begins again. BLACK - WHITE. DeKooning, Pollock, Kline. Something like but not like a relay race. The speed is deceptive. Time, being lateral, they pass each other on both the left and the right-hand sides. Now white. Now black. Now.

There's a knowing in Kline's paintings. That's Astor Place. That's Piccadilly Circus. The alley between the Tate and the Whitney. WHITE - BLACK. The city sleeps between deliveries. Try a four-inch brush. Dip it into the paint, load it up, and splash onto the canvas. Control it! Don't let the brush lose its paint until it's done its job. Move. Here comes More. Move. The city sleeps between deliveries. You can find Mr. Blue. You can find Mr. Kline. You can find the Black Forest and Kline's Formes Blanches (1955) recalling the city's texture. Brick. A slab of marble. Eggs over easy. A BLT. Formes Blanche. A whisky sour. A cab. The Third Avenue el. WHITE - BLACK. It builds. Roughness. A man's hands after he's used a four-inch brush.

Each city has a hotel for tourists, a night watch, a torch song. A place where Hell was never located. A pool. An M.G, a T.C. An augmented square. A cardinal robed in black and white. Austere humor that Degas and Sloan might appreciate. Around the corner, the city sleeps between deliveries. As Earl Kirkham (1890-1965) said at a Kline exhibition at the Eagan Gallery: "A cockeyed Mondrian."

It's a hard act to follow.

Grey

At Monet's funeral his casket was draped with a black cloth. Clemenceau, who loved Monet, removed the cloth and replaced it with a colored curtain, reminding everyone that Monet had said, "Black is not a color."

Matisse was a young man when he visited Renoir and showed some of his work. Renoir said he would never use black that way.

Did Monet and Renoir think of white as part of the natural world--and of black as something unnatural?

Black and white make grey. There's a hint of grey in Goya. Manet may be the first to have used grey as a color. Certainly Matisse used it--the mixture of black and white. Kline used it. Grey as a new thought. Vermeer used a pearl grey, but it's not a black and white mix--it's another color, another thought.

Was it the invention of the photograph with their grey compositions that brought Manet to grey? Degas was the first to work directly from a photograph. Consider it: the photograph is two-dimensional. A vapor for Cezanne to inhale and forget as he confronted his Mont Sainte-Victoire. Black and white become a new color. A color that neither comes from above or below the horizon. Grey floats and rejects nothing. Red - yellow - green - and blue will reject each other. But grey is a democratic gift, a social equal when so few things are equal. Grey. The lovers produce by accepting everything. The color wheel slows down. Red, yellow, blue, and green are seen differently. (Or was it Manet's progression--having looked at Spanish painting and then at photography?) The Bar at the Folies Bergere. The wheel turns again. Fast and faster. Grey stops floating and rejects purity--purity, the curse of the twentieth century.

Edouard Manet (1832-1883)

Before the Mirror (1876). A woman stands with her back to us. The mirror is in the shape of an arch and has depth. It might be a pool, and she might be walking into the pool. There are no reflections. She might be Artemis and we might be Actean surprising her in her pool. Will she turn us into a stag? Will she have us brought down? Or will she turn and smile? We don't know. Her right arm is crooked and its hand has become a trout.

Edouard Manet removed his top hat and his suede gloves. The hunt is about to begin. "External phenomena," as Ernest Chesneau was to call it in 1882 when he wrote of The Bar at the Folies Bergere. Suzon waits. Behind the bar at the Folies. Composed. Tired. She is being propositioned by an older man. Behind her there is a large mirror. Behind her. In the mirror. Men and women in their evening finery - *oui, oui*. The city. So many men. So many women. So many bottles. But only one Suzon.

Manet left nothing out. No saving for tomorrow. No fairy tales. Yesterday. Today. The mirror. The pool in its duality of color and lack of space. Suzon's chest. A black ribbon around her neck holds a pendant. There is more. Flowers in her cleavage. Lace, velvet, champagne, a chandelier. A city. A bracelet exaggerates her beautiful body. Like a city it holds together. Two flowers in a glass. Many oranges. Only Suzon's back and the older man do not sparkle. One brief interlude to the right side of the painting implies the purpose, imagined or real, for which all these people have come together. A city. One woman. One man. Many oranges. Women. Men. One structure. Many men. Many women. One Suzon. A proposition.

At the edge of the world where there are no boundaries and everything has become eatable, the seasons compete. Summer. Spring. Fall. Winter. The city takes nothing for granted. Be intent or be mad. OR--be Manet.

Poussin / Cezanne

Nicholas Poussin (1594-1665) adjusted his feet, his legs. Master of the arrangement: adjust the arms; find a method. Learn the classics and be prepared. The figures are serene. And there is no mess to contend with. Et in Arcadia Ego (Even in Arcady I am) -- I, Death, reign even in the idyllic dream, land of the pastorals, Arcady. In Arcady there is no room for King Louis XIV's extravaganzas. In Poussin's Arcady every figure looks as if it had rehearsed its part and said its lines over and over again. Every figure is serene, solid, and has no mess to contend with.

Paul Cezanne (1839-1906) saw this, internalized this, and looked at Mount Sainte-Victoire. He faced the wall and made the stones important. He was able to realize Poussin's depth. Poussin, the artist, had looked at the ancients and tested their worth against his knowledge. In the Greeks he found something he could rely on. And Cezanne loved this because it had been proven. He could rely on it. He would have to do something different to assure the figure and the stone of a place in his time. So the figure and the stone were not to move. They were to contend with space--space that had always been a negative between two jars evolved into a shape. And Poussin nodded, and Cezanne nodded, and space, as if it were silent, surrounded them and mastered the arrangement.

In 1866, Paul Cezanne painted portraits of his Uncle

Dominique with a pallet knife as his tool. The painter became ferocious.

Who will you fight?

Mother? Father?

Power.

Paint.

A lot of it.

Who will you fight?

Who will you fight?

No metaphor but a left and a right.

Who will you fight?

Monet?

"Monet is nothing but an eye, but what an eye!" said Paul
    Cezanne.

Turn to the left, turn to the right.

Who will you fight?

The thing that is as hard as a wall?

Something touches your toes.

You want it.

Who will you fight?

Not many.

Just a few.

Something touches your toes.

You want it.

You want the devotion.

Are you afraid?

No child is born without labor.

No birth is without grief.

Without.

No poem is without Zen.

If it is light that changes night to day, then it is light my voice finds. When I talk, figures clear their throats. When I open my mouth, I am beside myself. It's not that I'm afraid of Uncle Dominique, the paint, or the pallet knife. I am in transition. I'm in the midst of a changing digestion and I get angry because the distance between two jars is not always what I think it is. It moves and not always when I expect it to. It causes me to have sensations I do not understand--and mathematics tells me I must work on division and learn to compound that which is still unknown to me.

Uncle Dominique in profile? As a monk. As a lawyer. As paint. As a lot of paint. A lot of paint is on the canvas. The crust never dries. Body and background alike are troweled out of the same substance.

Monet has still to paint Haystacks, Rouen Cathedral, Waterlilies. But for Cezanne, a confrontation, a combination, a left and a right--no metaphor but a left, a right. . .

Claude Monet (1840 - 1926)

Woman With Umbrella, Turned to the Right: Attempt at Figure Painting Outdoors (1886). Woman With Umbrella, Turned to the Left: Attempt at Figure Painting Outdoors (1886).

The green umbrella attempts to shade her. We don't know who she is. She is female. Is she social? There is a dream that orbits these paintings. There is an insight into memory, an attempt by Monet to make this young woman what Monet wants her to be. The umbrella is green as in Woman With a Parasol: Madame Monet and Her Son (1875). Monet's wife Camille died September 5, 1879. Monet painted Camille on her deathbed. Mostly blue, she is taken into the Seine. She is dispersed by water, and she submerges. Does he now see the Seine as white?

In Woman with Umbrella, Turned to the Right: Attempt at Figure Painting Outdoors (1886) the sun covers the young woman's skirt as if the skirt were a pleated chalky rock. The wind carries her veil behind her. A red flower is in her waistband. She says nothing. She is Monet's stepdaughter, says Lilla Cabot Perry. Or is she half Camille? A memory of another day, another lovely young woman who used her umbrella to protect her face. Monet makes no attempt to show us her features, but we know she is beautiful. Is she obedient? Monet now turns her to the left. At the top of the hill, another green umbrella. A young woman who looks slightly heavier than the woman turned to the right stands and the wind comes

from behind her. She too wears a red flower in her waistband. She too wears a veil. Again, Monet makes no attempt to show us her features. But we know she is beautiful. The wind comes from behind and carries her veil. She is braced, and one wonders, will he turn her again? will he spin her like a top? will every side be evaluated? will he decide on a place for her? In his heart he can paint what he sees. In his artistry we can feel his attempt to catch her before she gets away.

Monet's young women are toons, cartoons, something almost
grotesque,
almost a ludicrous imitation.
Love, or other imitations, makes a travesty of that which it
represents.
Love whispers, blows in the wind, and lifts us up the hill
to the thing that is as hard as a wall.
Who will you fight?
Who will you fight?

Vincent Van Gogh (1853-1890)

The Celt has painted himself Blue.
Horse piss shapes his hair into a mane.
Now he paints. Now he writes.
"Beware of Pity." He will gnaw
at your veins and when you are
covered in blood he will turn
romantic and sing his song.

In the twelfth century there was a migration that went above the trees. The cathedral reached for the supernatural. Book illustration. Stained glass. Independence. No one need imitate the natural world. The distance between things was without perspective. The ornamental line became a composition of complex data. These masters of the twelfth century were mobile and they were able to experiment.

If it rains, there will be mud. Like softly falling rain, the gargoyle makes his sound. Unlike the East, where styles last for thousands of years, the West never knew immobility. It has always quickly consumed its creations. The West has always been in a rush. This fallibility confronts itself head on. And we are left to consider.

The Potato Eaters (April-May 1885). Van Gogh doesn't imitate the twelfth century masters as Gauguin does in The Yellow Christ four years later. But Van Gogh's narrative is as deliberate as those masters and he is closer to the twelfth century. Without taking, as Gauguin does, a Christ's body that could have been from a twelfth-century sculpture, Van Gogh mobilizes the story and is able to bring to an end a period of his life. He never lets the peasants speak. By giving himself permission to experiment, he joins the Impressionists without knowing them.

In 1885, he hadn't seen a Japanese print or been to Paris. To paint The Potato Eaters he pulls at his devotions as if they were roots from his ancestors, the kindling to light his subject is a tap on the shoulders from the past. And the twelfth century masters are brought forth and recognized. In a dark room, where there is no joy, the potato eaters pass tea and the painter refers his viewers to peasants eating potatoes.

Van Gogh believed that the soul could not contain evil, that there was no such thing as an evil soul. He believed Gauguin was a genius, a more accomplished painter than he was. He believed painters built their own cathedrals, that they are housed by their art, and that only art could truly translate justice from a blind abstraction into a wholesome wife. He believed and carried on his back all of nature's seasons.

Like softly falling rain.

It is paint. Why rush!

Black bird. Melts.

Why rush!

Vincent Van Gogh has melted and all that remains is a season. Paint. No knuckles. No bend in the fingers. The road is gone. Like softly falling rain. It is paint. Why rush! Black Bird. A hand melts. Why rush! Wheat Field with Crows (July, 1890). The land has lost its taste. The sky melts. Green is quick. The path hurries. WHY RUSH!

No body.

Can live.

On this earth.

Why rush!

No body can remain unappreciated.

No body can remain disappointed.

No body can remain alone.

Like softly falling rain - it is paint.

WHY RUSH! Beware of Pity. Like

softly falling rain. It is paint.

Why rush!

The Circuit

To go, travel, or move around; to compass; circulate.

The experience holds the instrument of choice. The thumb and its counterpart, the wheel, turns on its central axle and the thumb requests a ride. To go, travel, or move around; to compass, circulate. The circuit goes to each painting and charges it. Like the spokes on a wheel. It is my pleasure to bring disparate things together. To cover them and to hold them in both hands. It is my pleasure to throw a gauntlet down in front of beauty and immerse it in its counterpart. Then, when the edge is found, begin again.

The Dance at the Moulin Rouge, The Deep, Woman in Blue Reading a Letter, Uncle Dominque as a Monk, Arcady. Hang them on a wall side by side. The paintings won't lose and we gain the scent. The fact is, nothing will get lost. Logic is not only for the linear. Betrothal and Nature Morte; Seawatcher and Formes Blanches. See how devotion repeats itself in forms that give new meaning to place.

From

A PAINTER'S BESTIARY

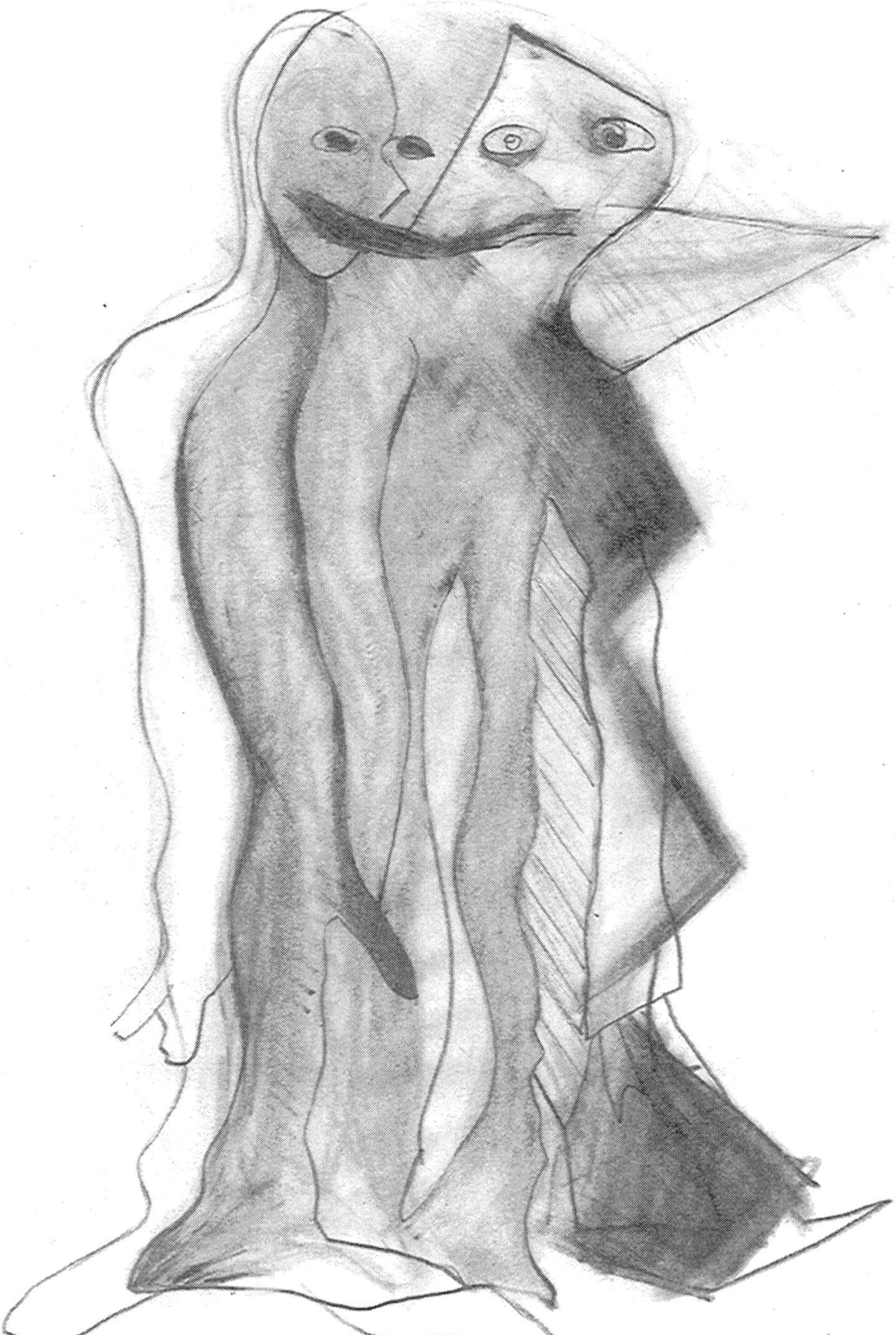

Portrait of D.M., Paris, October 9, 1942 (1942)

Pablo Picasso

The muse is so strong
                    it will help me paint
my mother is dying
                    and wants to take me for herself

I don't want a hard erection
I will not fuck my mother

              I will call on the muse to be forgiven

We women have waited so long   to paint

                    from the abstract
                        to the figure, from the figure
to the abstract makes an edge
of exquisite distance and distance
                    gives us our sensations

                              until this war is over
                              craft defeats corruption

Portrait of D.M, Paris, October 9, 1942 (1942)

Pablo Picasso

I'm

so sorry

you're dying

inside me

there is

a space

for you

a desperate

space that

wanted you

to mother

me

until this war is over
craft defeats corruption

Portrait of D.M., Paris, October 9, 1942 (1942)

Pablo Picasso

This woman's dying mother
wants her daughter's body
to suffer chest pains. The daughter rises
as a man with a hard erection.
She fucks her mother. To paint
from the abstract
to the figure. From the figure
to the abstract makes an edge
of exquisite distance and distance
gives us our sensations.

until this war is over
craft defeats corruption.

Red, Brown & Black (1958)

Mark Rothko

I know a man
who says

"I will go to hell
to hear sweet laughter"

I know a man
who licks his lips
every time he smiles

I know a man
who eats chicken
with his fingers

I know a man
who says

"If you are
an out-sider
you must study
very hard and
learn to do it"

The Room (1954-55)

Philip Guston

When I stop thinking about ART
I think about money
a junk yard of my own
where kids can take on the world
in terms that are understandable.
I know other people have secrets
but mine are such a burden
no matter how hard I try to reduce
the load, more begets more, now it's
winter and I'm in the process of drying
out pounds of cheap paint, just to get
the pigment onto the canvas drains
a generation of jews.

Gotham News (1955)
Willem de Kooning

You weren't there when
they were handing out
the prizes and all your
awards went to an unnamed
source. In this city
you have to be on time,
even if you love ART.
Everything that hasn't
been named is on the
street. You pay your
rent. Buy a new shirt.
Paint on canvas and
drink Four Roses
with an older man
who reads the newspaper
before he paints.

No. 20 (1949)
Bradley Walker Tomlin

Bob's getting his hair cut
by Fred, who wants Emma
to meet him, on the corner of
Vine and Main, money is exchanged

The Borden's lost their daughter
to a family who have been printing
newspapers since Abraham Lincoln
and Mary Todd moved to the White House

During the Civil War
both sides served American food
and gassed up at the intersection

Vern the service station attendant
married Martha and their two boys
got educated and moved away

The creature keep changing
I'm not complaining, but,
it's hard to tell the newcomers
there's more to art

Clown with Green Cap (1925-29)

Georges Rouault

If Christ is in every man
then there is a man
in the audience

wishing he too had carried
          the cross

Abstraction (1926)

Georgia O'Keeffe

I drive my car
between bones
I understand
what breeding is
when history speaks
culture is exposed

Water Lilies (1920)

Claude Monet

why! Lily why!

when I kiss you
you run and clothe
yourself in portents

why! when my motif
is amorous
do you arrive
with an audience

why! Lily why!

Home Scene (1871)

Thomas Eakins

My swollen breasts

fill the cupped hands of a man
who measures his love
by compromising
he is conditioned to have unhappiness

my daughter

I am jealous
you will practice sex knowing
there is no truth but
the half-truth that contains fantasies

my daughter

I am a practical woman
I believe in relationships
civil descriptions of what
we are doing when we come

The Yellow Christ (1889)

Paul Gauguin

This Jew's name is Jesus
his father is a carpenter
he came amongst us and told us a tale
that we thought was pornographic
and would get us in a lot of trouble.
So we listened and did nothing.
I guess we were wrong.
Powerful men thought him bad trouble
and framed it so he would be crucified.
We're sorry, you know, we've
begun to realize what he tried to do
and we love him.

Marilyn Monroe (1964)

Andy Warhol

Oh! Yes,
certainly, color
Blue, yes, green is worth millions
                marriage,
definitely a winner,
photos of you, yes, don't worry
you're so kind, yes, it's important,
to cream your skin, french fries,
France, Bardot, yes,
I pay my bills, furs in summer,
Arthur Miller, ball players,
cook in winter, big hands,
going to China, yes, I knew my mother
no, I was never lonely

Woman with a Basket (1927)

Juan Gris

The cube.

3x3 divided by three = 2
times the power dissolves the image
into classical combinations.
I am my mother's son and
the color of her is Spanish architecture.

2x2x2 = 6 times the figure is turned
to resemble a basket.

The poet's accomplished vocabulary
has three Verbs and three Nouns
three Adverbs and three Adjectives

Every third child has a third chance.

1x1x1x1x1x1 = six people referred to the
same circumstance as meaning

The Fox Trot
    moves
    freely
    around
    the object

Sunset on the Sea (1872)

John Frederick Kensett

in my ears   the mermaids
breathe   in my solitude
the hard edge   sleeps
beware   my friends
there is no   void
you   like I
will account   to the orient
whether   you shoulder
the sky   or let it be
you will cross   the meridian
and divide   what is free?

Drawing (circa 1955)

Cy Twombly

Every day Billy scratched
on the walls of the house
where he lived and when
all the walls and floors
and ceilings had been covered
he bought paper and crayons
and paint and when the house
in which he lived was full of
paper he moved and started
all over again and when his
neighbors realized that Billy
Boy was going to come into
their houses and cover their
walls they called the patron
saint of painters St. Luke and
he came and put his hand on
Billy's shoulder and told him
about vernacular and how what
once was thrown away was now
valued and how he Billy could
demonstrate that trivia can
make a perfect picture and
that he Billy could become
his own object and live in
the world as a beautiful song

New Moon (1945)

George Ault

LOBELIA
LOBELIA

come sleep with me
I am already dead

LOBELIA
LOBELIA

haven't I told you
"Something would happen"

a prize
a sale
a lot of money

a dream we two tip-toed through
like two lips parting
there in the darkness
where loneliness forgives
the author's contempt
consummation erects a structure
a scaffold surrounds
the sublime and we
are able to sleep together

A Pair of Boots (1887)

Vincent Van Gogh

As a piece of fruit   gotten old
regurgitated   for you   my body
sows lines   as in a Japanese print
obedience blossoms   to the expected
spring   waiting to be accepted
wishing emotion   a reverence for
one's parents   a conceit that polite
social behavior rationalizes   counts on
saves for   those rainy days when
you need new boots   your feet cannot
forgive   your mind is an altar
a wretched sequel   God's work
brings so little bread
so little is ours
so continuous is our inheritance
so close is our shadow
so protracted is the method that kills us

Wood Interior (1932-35)

Emily Carr

Men whisper as they hunt
they cover their tracks
with thistle
and a malice
toward Sappho
exsplains
the darkness

Men whisper as they hunt
they cover their tracks
with thistle
and a malice
toward Sappho
exsplains
the darkness

Men whisper as they hunt
they cover their tracks
with thistle
and a malice
toward Sappho
exsplains
the darkness

Basil King is a painter and poet. He was born in London in 1935, and moved to Detroit, Michigan just after World War II. He was a student at Black Mountain College in his early teens and, later, founder/editor of *Mulch* magazine. His most recent paintings and drawings are incorporated in his "Mirage" project, which has been performed in the U.S., Europe, and the U.K. He lives and works in Brooklyn, New York.

Other books of King's work from Stop Press include *The Complete Miniatures* and *Seventeen Walking Sticks*. Please inquire of your bookseller.

Designed in the United States
Computer typesetting in Bauer Bodoni and
Franklin Gothic Bold

Printed in Great Britain by CPI